RAMA

RAMA

RAMA

RAMA

RAMA

RAMA

RAMA

RAMA

RAMA

RAMA

RAMA

RAMA

RAMA
RAMA
RAMA

RAMA

Gandhi Searches for Truth

A Practical Biography for Children

Stephanie N. Van Hook

Illustrations: Sergio Garzon

PERSON POWER
PRESS

ISBN: 978-0-9978676-1-9

Library of Congress Control Number: 2016948634

The Metta Center for Nonviolence, founded in 1982, promotes the study and practice of nonviolence worldwide. Person Power Press, a project of the Metta Center for Nonviolence, publishes books on how to understand nonviolence and use it more safely and more effectively.

For more information please write to:
The Metta Center for Nonviolence, Box 98, Petaluma, California, 94953
On the web at www.mettacenter.org

Design by Miroslava Sobot, www.mika-art.com

For My Beloved Teacher, Sri Eknath Easwaran
And Amira, Carter, Liam, and Raegan

Table of Contents

Author's Note

I apologize to children for writing this book about a grown-up. But I have an important reason: before Mahatma Gandhi was a grown-up, he was a child, like you. He had parents and siblings. He played with his friends and helped with household chores and family duties. He loved to hear stories, especially ones that could teach him something about life. One of his favorite stories was about a boy who had very old parents. The boy, loving his parents so much, carried them to all of the sacred places in India on his shoulders! Our Gandhi was not that strong physically. But his heart grew to be one of the strongest in all the world.

I have another reason: this grown-up believed that all of us have a power inside of us that works best when we direct it toward helping and loving others unconditionally. Children, he believed, have access to this power as much as grown-ups do, if not more. He did not think that you have to wait until you are older to make the world a better place for everyone—you can start right now. Try to do things all day that help other people. They do not have to notice what you've done because that doesn't matter. Loving service is its own reward. You might be surprised to feel your heart grow stronger day by day until one day you find, as Gandhi did, the secret to life: love for everyone, no matter what.

Stephanie Van Hook
July 2016
Petaluma, California

This story is about Gandhi's search for Truth,
and how he learned to use nonviolence.
It began when he was just a child...

A Great Adventure Begins

I claim to be a votary of truth from my early childhood.[1]

When Mohandas K. Gandhi was a little boy, a desire began to awaken within his heart: he wanted to discover Truth.

Truth is not an easy thing to find. It is not something that you taste or touch, like a ripe, red apple. It is not something that you smell with your nose or hear with your ears or see with your eyes or even think with your mind. We discover Truth with our heart.

There is a very old story that says that Truth was placed in the heart of everyone and everything. It is not outside of us. We have to look for it inside. Those who have found it say that it lives within us in a place where there is nothing to hear, nothing to taste, nothing to smell, nothing to touch, nothing to see, nothing even to think. It can be found by people who want it more than anything else, because when they find Truth, they receive a beautiful gift: the power to help the whole world. That's exactly what Gandhi wanted.

Gandhi Learns a Mantram

When a child, my nurse taught me to repeat Rama whenever I felt afraid or miserable, and it has been second nature with me with growing knowledge and advancing years.[2]

Just because someone sets out to find Truth does not mean that they are never afraid of anything. It does not mean that they do not sometimes worry or feel sad and cry. Young Gandhi was a seeker of Truth, but he was also afraid of many things: not only snakes, of which there were many in India, but also of people and what they would think of him. He was scared that others might not want to be his friend.

Seeing that Gandhi wanted to help others but was troubled by all these fears, his nurse, a young woman named Rambha, gave him a mantram, a special word that he could use all day long to help him calm his mind and body: Rama. It means "joy."

Even as a grown-up, when he became afraid or angry, he would repeat this word and it would bring him a great feeling of peace:

> Rama Rama Rama Rama Rama Rama Rama Rama Rama Rama
> Rama Rama Rama Rama Rama Rama Rama Rama Rama Rama
> Rama Rama Rama Rama Rama Rama

Just like that! Sometimes he said it out loud. Sometimes he sang it. Other times, he said it quietly in his heart.

Anyone who wants to be peaceful—and anyone who loves Gandhi—can use this very special word to help them become more courageous, loving, compassionate, and kind.

Learning the Power of Cooperation and Non-cooperation

The highest honor my friends can do me is to enforce in their own lives the programme that I stand for or to resist me to their utmost if they do not believe in it.[3]

Gandhi's mother's name was Putlibai, and he loved her with all his heart. When she would go to meet important people in town who needed her advice, Gandhi would never want to stay home with his siblings—he preferred to go with her, to stay near her always, and she was happy to bring him along. Gandhi's mother taught him about nonviolence, because she showed through her own example how to be both gentle and deeply determined. When she made a decision to do something kind and helpful, she would stick to it, and no one could change her mind.

She also taught him that we can offer non-cooperation to anyone, including grown-ups when necessary. One time, he had to non-cooperate with his mother when she told him not to play with a certain friend. There was a superstition, a way of thinking that was not true, that said his friend was inferior and should not even be touched. Gandhi did not cooperate with her because he knew that all human beings are worthy of kindness, respect, dignity, and compassion. Gandhi played with his friend and non-cooperated with his mother because he loved her. He felt in his heart that even grown-ups could make mistakes, and just because he was a child did not mean that he had to do something harmful or hurtful to someone else. He wanted to show her another way.

Cooperation and non-cooperation are two very important ideas for anyone seeking Truth. Cooperation means to work for the welfare of everyone by choosing to work together with others. No one can force you to cooperate with them and you cannot force others to cooperate with you. If you do, that's coercion, not cooperation.

Non-cooperation means choosing not to work with others because what they are doing is not for the benefit of everyone. We non-cooperate with others when we see that they are making a mistake and we want to show them another way. We are against what they are doing, not against them. We offer non-cooperation out of love. Gandhi's mother understood his action, and she loved him more and more every day.

The Power of Honesty and Gentleness

When Ahimsa becomes all-embracing, it transforms everything it touches. There is no limit to its power.[4]

Seekers of Truth like Gandhi need a lot of power to help the whole world. One such power is ahimsa, or gentleness. Ahimsa means gentleness in our thoughts, in our words, and in our actions. It means treating everything with love and dignity: even snakes and spiders. Even plants. Especially human beings. This gentleness in our heart makes us and others feel very safe and very loved.

Gandhi discovered the power of ahimsa through his father, Kaba Gandhi. It happened when young Gandhi and a friend were making some bad choices and it was making them very unhappy. They were taking things that belonged to others and hiding what they were doing. They were afraid of getting into trouble. Finally, young Gandhi became so unhappy and he thought of a way out: Truth! He decided to tell his father what he had done by writing him a letter. His father was a strong man, and Gandhi did not know how he would react when he heard what his son had done. He expected to be punished. Instead, Gandhi's father started crying because he was so proud of his son for telling the truth. He was very gentle. When Gandhi saw that his father was gentle when he could have been so angry, he learned that gentleness can touch a person's heart and transform it forever. Gandhi never stole or lied again.

Lessons from Kasturbai

Love and exclusive possession can never go together.[5]

If we love someone and want them to be our friend, we cannot tell them what to do. We have to let them make their own choices, to cooperate and non-cooperate with them if necessary, and to love them no matter what.

Gandhi learned this lesson when he met his lifelong friend—and future wife—Kasturbai. She was older than him by one year. When Gandhi was still very young, he thought that Kasturbai should play with him and love him alone and no one else. He wanted her to do everything his way.

But she would not cooperate with any unkindness. She was not afraid that Gandhi would stop being her friend if she did not do what he wanted. Even while refusing his demands, she remained kind to him. This is nonviolence: we refuse to be mean to someone who is being mean or bossy to us. Kindness and dignity, even when someone is not kind or respectful to us, is a source of strength for ourselves and others. Maybe those who are being unkind have not yet learned how to be kind to everyone. We can help each other learn the power of love by not accepting disrespect, and by not offering it in return.

The Law of Love

I believe in the sovereign rule of the law of love which makes no distinctions.[6]

Our planet Earth has seven continents: North America, South America, Africa, Europe, Asia, Australia, and Antarctica. India, where Gandhi grew up, is in Asia, but he grew up at a time when England, which is on the European continent, ruled over people who lived on other continents. The British (people from England, Ireland, Scotland, and Wales) brought their rules, laws, and education with them to India. The Indian people did not like being coerced to follow these customs, but they did not know what to do to get the British to go away.

Meanwhile, Gandhi's family sent him to London, England to study British law.

When Gandhi arrived in England, he noticed that everything was very different from India—there were different foods, different clothing, different pastimes. Because he was vegetarian, he had to learn how to cook his own meals; and because he was alone, he had to make new friends. At the same time, he devoted himself to his study of the law.

While Gandhi was studying British laws in books, he was learning another lesson about law: the law of love in his heart. He learned that the law of love is the highest of all laws because all life depends on it, not just a single country. He learned that even though people come from different countries and continents, have different religions, speak different languages, dress differently, eat different foods, and play different games, we share something in common: we all have dignity. We all desire to give and receive love; and everyone's life matters.

He did not know that he would one day become a Mahatma, or a "great soul," and help free the Indian people from the rule of the British without violence. He did not know that he would come back to London one day as the leader of the Indian Freedom Struggle. All he knew was that when the time came for him to board the ship back to India to see his family, his heart was crying out with joy: *At last.* Just like anyone who has not seen their family in a long time, he missed them!

Gandhi Arrives in South Africa

The path of nonviolence requires much more courage than violence.[7]

Not long after returning to India from his law studies in England, Gandhi had to travel to South Africa for work. He had never been to South Africa. He did not know what it would be like. The experience, he thought, might teach him something new.

Both he and his family were disappointed that he had to leave them behind again and travel alone. He made friends with fellow travelers on the way to his third continent.

When Gandhi arrived in South Africa, he noticed something very sad. People from Europe and those with white skin were treating those with brown and black skin with disrespect. Gandhi was surprised. It hurt him to see this. He knew it was hurting everyone, not only those who were being hurt, but those who were being unkind to them.

One time, when he went to work at a courthouse, the judge told him that he could not wear his Indian turban, or hat, in the courtroom. Gandhi refused to take it off, and used non-cooperation. He would not let someone treat Indians or anyone unfairly. With courage and strength, he walked out of the courtroom because he would rather lose his work than his dignity.

The newspapers told his story and many people began to pay attention to him. They began to be drawn to his nonviolence.

The Lesson of Anger

I have learned through bitter experience the one supreme lesson to conserve my anger, and as heat conserved is transmuted into energy, even so our anger controlled can be transmuted into a power that can move the world.[8]

Truth can find us anywhere. It found our Gandhi on the platform of a railway station in Pietermaritzburg, South Africa. He had been thrown off a train and onto the platform because a European passenger felt that an Indian should not be allowed to sit in first class. After Gandhi was pushed off the train, his bag came bouncing down the train stairs, landing next to him. It was nighttime. He noticed his whole body was shaking, but it was not because of the cold. He was shaking with anger. His heart was racing. He decided he would spend the entire night on the platform because he did not want to be insulted again by the ticket agent inside the station.

That night, Gandhi learned a valuable lesson: he could use his anger and transform it into nonviolent power. Anger is like a fire. It can either burn us or we can light a candle with it.

"This is why I was born," he thought. "This is what I've been working toward since I was a little child."

At that moment Gandhi began to experiment with what he later called "satyagraha." It means to grasp and hold tightly to Truth. Another way to describe it is Truth-force. He would challenge injustice, but he would not use violence for this fight—not in his words, his thoughts, or his spirit.

Remembering the lessons from his mother and his wife, he told people that there would be nothing in the world that anyone could do to him that would make him use violence against them. Then, he took a vow, making a promise that he would dedicate his life to using nonviolence. As time went on, many heard Gandhi and agreed with him. They made the same promise of bravery. They would use their creativity, not their violence.

Gandhi knew that his job was to bring satyagraha back to India. He knew it could help his country get freedom and show the whole world how this great power works.

From Mohandas to Mahatma

My life is an indivisible whole, and all my activities run into one another; and they all have their rise in my insatiable love of humanity.[9]

When Gandhi returned to India, the land of his childhood, thousands of people were waiting to see him. They had heard about his nonviolent resistance and satyagraha in South Africa. They wanted to help him in his mission. People began calling him "Mahatma," which means "great soul." Gandhi did not like that name because he felt that he was an ordinary person. Nonviolence, he knew, is for everyone, not for only a few special people.

Gandhi knew that in order to help India free herself from the British without violence, the people would need to find the power in themselves, just as he had. They needed work. He showed people how to spin cotton on the spinning wheel and on a hand-spindle called a "takli." It was massive, collective, and creative resistance.

Gandhi figured out that by reducing their dependency on the British, they could free themselves from British control. By spinning cotton, they could make their own cloth as they had done before the British came. When they were no longer dependent on British cloth, it would help them get free of British rule. They could make their own clothes and they could rule their own country. Even children joined Gandhi and helped to spin cotton and weave "khadi," or homespun cotton cloth.

It was needed work. It helped people to concentrate and focus their attention on one thing at a time. It brought harmony to their mind, body, and spirit. It was something they could all work on together, so it strengthened their communities. Most importantly, it was nonviolent; it harmed no one. Nonviolence helps everyone; whenever we use it, it helps us and the people opposing us. Even the British needed to learn that by exploiting India, they were hurting themselves.

Chapter 10

The Salt March

I present a weapon not of the weak but of the brave.[10]

Gandhi grew up in a city right near the ocean. When he was a young man, he had the chance of traveling on ocean liners across the vast waters of our planet to discover that all human beings are one family.

One time during the Indian Freedom Struggle, Gandhi came up with a way to show the Indian people that they were free from the British even before the British took leave of India. Gandhi and his friends had been practicing nonviolence with all their heart day and night. The idea was to reclaim the salt of India using nonviolence.

The British took India's salt and sold it back to them, just as they did with cloth. Gandhi and his friends wanted to show that they would no longer let the British steal their resources. They walked from their community all the way to the sea, almost 240 miles away, where they could gather their own salt. As they walked, they sang songs, spun khadi, repeated their mantrams, and kept their spirits cheerful. Since they were not allowed to gather salt, they were committing what is known as civil disobedience, or non-cooperation against an unfair law.

When they arrived at the shore near the town of Dandi, they were now a group of thousands. Gandhi stepped forward and grabbed a handful of salt and sand. He raised it for everyone to see, and people cheered and sang. They began to pick up salt themselves to sell.

The British jailed thousands of people for this act of civil disobedience. The world was watching and had never seen anything like it before. The satyagrahis, or those following nonviolent resistance, did not use any violence, while the British forces did, because they did not know about nonviolence.

After a while the satyagrahis turned their attention to the Dharsana salt works, a kind of factory where the salt from the ocean was turned into salt for people to eat. The British refused to let them in, and tried to drive them away with their sticks. The satyagrahis were getting badly hurt, but they would not go home, nor would they hit back. On this day, the people of India knew that they would soon be independent from British rule, because it was their nonviolence that made them free.

It would take seventeen more years of nonviolence before the British would let India rule itself. Nonviolence and patience go hand in hand.

Back to England

My goal is friendship with the world and I can combine the greatest love with the greatest opposition to wrong.[11]

Gandhi found himself on an ocean liner once more. Now he was going back to the European continent. No longer a young student, this time he came as a representative of the Indian people, wearing a traditional Indian dhoti made out of cotton the people in India had spun all by themselves, and a pair of sandals that he made himself. He was invited by the British to be part of a conference, and his plan was to convince the British government to give India her freedom. Most of all, though, he wanted them to stay friends. This is the magic of nonviolence.

Gandhi had learned when he was young, and he believed from the bottom of his heart, that it was not enough to be kind and show empathy to those we like; we must also be kind and compassionate to people who are unkind and mean to us. This is how we test our nonviolence.

While in England, he did something very brave: he went to talk with a group of cloth mill workers who were very angry at him because the nonviolent movement in India had made them lose their jobs at the mill in England. He spoke to them with firmness and Truth, directly from his heart, about how Indian people—and all people—needed their freedom. The mill workers listened. They thought he would be mean to them, but his nonviolence surprised them. By the end of the conversation they were cheering for him and the Indian people with cries of happiness. They changed their minds: they wanted the Indian people to be free, and they were very proud of gentle Gandhi for his tireless, good work.

Gandhi was proud and happy for them too. In nonviolence, we try to help everyone get what they need, even our opponents, even those who don't like us. This is the path of Truth.

It was this spirit of Truth and nonviolence that led to India's independence in 1947.

Chapter 12

Carrying on Gandhi's Message

The heart's earnest and pure desire is always fulfilled.[12]

Before he was a grown-up called a Mahatma, before he led a nonviolent movement for a more fair South Africa and a free India, Gandhi was a child, who like yourself, wanted to live in peace, security, and happiness. So, he went on a search for Truth. When he found it, he learned that it lives in his own heart—as well as in the heart of each and every one of us.

Gandhi never forgot that his search for Truth began when he was a little boy, and he knew how wise and special children are. He cared very deeply for children all around the world; this is why he chose nonviolence. He did not want to see children learn violence or be harmed by it. He wanted all children and grown-ups to learn how to practice nonviolence.

He even said that nonviolence can best be learned not from grown-ups, but from children like yourself. In fact, when he met the great Italian peace educator Maria Montessori he said, "If we want peace in the world, we will have to begin with the children."

Nonviolence is hard work. It takes time and a lot of practice. At the end of Gandhi's life, he was still learning about its power! We have to practice with our families, our friends, our schoolmates, and even those who don't like us. We will make mistakes, but we can try again—and let others try again when they make mistakes. We are trying to learn to love everyone unconditionally because we all have dignity.

Gandhi's search for Truth transformed him and the world we live in. He had no doubt that all of us could do the same, as long as we bring to this challenge the same dedication and devotion that he did. If we want to help everyone, and if we want to end violence, we can also become Mahatmas who benefit the whole world.

Glossary of Big Ideas

A

AHIMSA: Ahimsa is a Sanskrit word that means "not harming," or nonviolence. It is not a negative term: we try to nurture and care for people instead of harming them. It means being gentle.

C

CIVIL DISOBEDIENCE: Civil disobedience means non-cooperation with an unjust law. We offer it with kindness and determination.

COMPASSION: Compassion means caring about others. When we discover compassion in our heart, we cannot hurt others, because we care about what happens to them.

COOPERATION: Cooperation means working with people when we see what they are doing is helping others. Cooperation cannot be forced onto others, otherwise, that is called "coercion."

D

DIGNITY: Dignity means being worthy of love and respect. People, animals, and plants have dignity. Our greatest challenge as human beings is to increase and honor the dignity of all of life.

E

EMPATHY: Empathy means understanding and sharing the feelings of someone else.

L

LOVE: Love is a skill that can be developed to help the world. We all have the capacity to learn how to love everyone.

M

MAHATMA: Mahatma means "great soul," and it stems from *maha*, great and *atma*, soul. It is a title given in India to people who have discovered within their hearts a great treasure chest of empathy, compassion, and ahimsa and who want to share it with others.

MANTRAM: A mantram is a word that a person will repeat, usually silently to themselves, that helps them to become calm, compassionate, and loving. Gandhi's mantram was *Rama*, joy.

N

NON-COOPERATION: Non-cooperation means refusing to help people do something harmful. It is an expression of love and strength, and it can be used by anyone.

NONVIOLENCE: Nonviolence is a power that arises when we transform fear, greed, and anger into constructive energy such as love, generosity, and compassion. It makes people safe and is the remedy for violence in our world. It means offering dignity.

S

SATYAGRAHA: Satya means "Truth" and agraha means "holding onto." Pronounced SAH TEE AHH GRAH HA. It means holding firmly to Truth and gentleness. It means resisting what is wrong by showing people the way of love. A person who uses satyagraha is called a *satyagrahi*, pronounced SAH TEE AHH GRAH HEE.

T

TRUTH: Truth means what is real, or reality. Everyone has a piece of the Truth: no one is always right or always wrong. Finding Truth means finding what is real in all of us.

U

UNCONDITIONAL: Without limits. When we love unconditionally, nothing can take away that love, ever. Unconditional love is a powerful force in our world.

References

1 Harijan, August 9, 1942

2 Harijan, August 17, 1934

3 Young India, June 12, 1924

4 Autobiography

5 The Modern Review, October 1935

6 Harijan, May 25, 1947

7 Harijan, August 4, 1946

8 Young India, September 15, 1920

9 Harijan, March 2, 1934

10 Harijan, October 15, 1938

11 Young India, March 10, 1930

12 Harijan, August 9, 1942

13 Harijan, July 20, 1935

About the
Metta Center for Nonviolence

Nonviolence is the greatest power at the disposal of humankind.[13]

Person Power Press is a project of the
Metta Center for Nonviolence

THE METTA CENTER FOR NONVIOLENCE is a 501(c)3 organization that provides educational resources on the safe and effective use of nonviolence, with the recognition that it's not about putting the right person in power but awakening the right kind of power in people. We advance a higher image of humankind while empowering people to explore the question: How does nonviolence work, and how can I actively contribute to a happier, more peaceful society?

Our Mission

We encourage people in all walks of life to discover their innate capacity for nonviolence and to use its power strategically for the long-term transformation of themselves and the world, focusing on the root causes of injustice, competition, and violence. We aim to make the logic, history, and yet-unexplored potential of nonviolence more accessible to activists and agents of cultural change (which ultimately includes all of us).

Values & Vision

Our core values grow from the power that it is our privilege to explore—nonviolence: responsibility, human dignity, compassion, respect for all life.

We envision a world transformed by an awareness of the true potential of every human being, where all of life is sacred and where all our social systems work in harmony with the earth. We see a world in which conflict rarely occurs, and when it does, can always be addressed by the creative energy of nonviolence. In this world, unarmed peacekeeping has replaced military intervention, restorative justice has replaced retribution, and needs-based economies have replaced consumerism, among other essential changes.

In fulfillment of this vision, we uphold five propositions:

1. Life is an interconnected whole of inestimable worth

2. We cannot be fulfilled by an indefinite consumption of things, but by an expansion of our relationships

3. We can never injure others without injuring ourselves, therefore:

4. Security does not come from locking up "criminals" or defeating "enemies;" it can only come from rehabilitating offenders and turning enemies into friends

5. We are body, mind, and spirit.

Find out more about our programs
by visiting our website:

www.mettacenter.org

PERSON POWER
PRESS

About the Author

Stephanie N. Van Hook is the Executive Director of the Metta Center for Nonviolence. Trained in Montessori Early Childhood Education (ages 3-6), she earned her M.A. in Conflict Resolution from Portland State University, and her B.A. in French and Philosophy at Mary Washington College. From 2005-2007, she lived in Benin, West Africa as a United States Peace Corps Volunteer. She writes regularly for progressive news channels, and has several published chapters on topics ranging from atonement to a nonviolent response to domestic violence. A principle columnist on Metta Center's Daily Metta—a thought for the day on Gandhi's wisdom for our times—she is also the creator of a Parent Power Podcast, a tool for parents to learn the skills of nonviolence that children need from us, and the host of Peace Paradigm Radio—an FM radio program and podcast about how nonviolence works. A meditator, in her free time she teaches at Montessori, spins cotton, and weaves, all in the Gandhian spirit.

This is her first book.

About the Illustrator

Artist Sergio Garzon was born in Bogota, Colombia, and lives and works in Honolulu, Hawai'i. His paintings and prints consist of abstract figurative narratives of his memories in Colombia focusing on people, culture and the politics of history. Sergio Garzon is also project coordinator of PRINT BIGGER, a community-driven event that is helping break down the barriers between the studio, the gallery, and the public by taking the process out onto the streets for everyone to engage with. Currently Sergio Garzon teaches sketchbook classes at the Honolulu Museum of art School and manages his online illustration job during his free time.

Draw a picture of Mahatma Gandhi here.

Draw a picture of yourself here.

Gandhi's mantram was Rama.
Use this space to write **RAMA** as many times as you can!

Add color and decorations around Gandhi's mantram!

RAMA

CPSIA information can be obtained
at www.ICGtesting.com
Printed in the USA
BVOW07s1746290916

463657BV00001B/1/P

9 780997 867619